7/03   2/06   3/07 11/08 6/09
YTD-0   2   0   0   0
LC-1   5   7   7   7

2002

SMART ABOUT
History

NEGRO LEAGUES
ALL-BLACK BASEBALL

by Emily Brooks

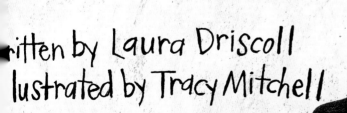

written by Laura Driscoll
Illustrated by Tracy Mitchell

For the many Negro League players who are not mentioned in this book—L.D.

To Madison—T.M.

Cover and p. 30, 31. National Baseball Hall of Fame Library, Cooperstown, N.Y.; p. 4, (top) Steve Gregory, (bottom)ticket stub courtesy of National Baseball Hall of Fame Library, Cooperstown, N.Y.; p. 5, 6, 12, 13, 18, 20, 21, 23, 28 (bottom). ; p. 7, David Roth; p. 10, Leonard Freed/Magnum Photos; p. 24, AP/Wide World Photo; p. 28, (top) AP/Wide World Photo

Library of Congress Cataloging-in-Publication Data
Driscoll, Laura.
The Negro leagues / by Laura Driscoll.
p. cm. – (Smart about history)
Summary: Presents a history of the Negro leagues, in the form of a school report written by a young girl after a visit to the National Baseball Hall of Fame.
1. Negro leagues–History–Juvenile literature. 2. African American baseball players–Juvenile literature. 3. Baseball–United States–History–Juvenile literature.
[1. Negro leagues. 2. African Americans. 3. Baseball players. 4. Baseball–History.]
I. Title. II. Series
GV875.A1 D75 2002
796.35764'08996073–dc21   2001040990

ISBN 0-448-42684-6 (pbk) A B C D E F G H I J
ISBN 0-448-42821-0 (GB)   A B C D E F G H I J

From the desk of

Ms. Brandt

Dear Class,
   We have been learning about so many exciting events from the past. Now you may choose a subject that is of special interest to you for your report.
   You may write about something that happened thousands of years ago or about something that happened not so very long ago - maybe when your parents or your grandparents were your age. It's up to you!

   Here are some questions you might want to think about:

🍎 What made you pick your topic?

🍎 Did you learn anything that really surprised you?

   Good luck and have fun!
                                    Ms. Brandt

The Baseball Hall of Fame

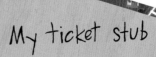

Mom Dad me

I love baseball. I know a lot about it. But before last fall, I had never heard of the Negro Leagues. Then my family went to the National Baseball Hall of Fame and Museum in Cooperstown, New York. A whole room there is about the Negro Leagues.

Did you know there was a time when black baseball players were not allowed in the major leagues? That's the way it was from about 1900 to 1947. So black players started their own teams and their own leagues.

My ticket stub

Just think. If Ken Griffey Jr or Barry Bonds had played back in the 1930s, they wouldn't have been on major-league teams. It's hard to believe, but it's true.

Before 1869, baseball was just a game for fun—not a job. Hardly anyone got paid to play baseball. Then professional teams got started. But if you were black, most of the teams did not want you.

This photo is from the late 1800s. It did not matter how good these players were. They could not play on pro teams.

THE EARLY DAYS

Bud Fowler and his team

In the 1870s and the 1880s, a few black baseball players did get to play on pro teams. But it doesn't sound to me like they had very much fun. Here are two of the players I learned about at the Baseball Hall of Fame.

Bud Fowler joined a white team in 1872. They say he invented shin guards because all the white players kept spiking him.

George Washington Stovey was a pitcher. In 1887, the New York Giants wanted to hire him. But another team said they wouldn't play against the Giants if they hired Stovey. After that, the owners of all the teams made a deal. They agreed that nobody would hire black players. And that was it.

My best friend Sarah and I play Little League Baseball. I am glad nothing keeps us from playing together.

ALL-BLACK BASEBALL

There were a lot of great black baseball players. So they started their own teams. The all-black teams would go from town to town looking for other teams to play. Sometimes they'd play three games in three different towns in one day. This was called barnstorming. Because the black teams didn't get crowds as big as the white teams, this was the only way they could make enough money.

The Page Fence Giants rode through towns on bikes to get people to come to their games.

The All-American Black Tourists would walk through a town in top hats and fancy coats. They said they'd even play all dressed up if another team wanted them to.

For a long time, black people couldn't go in stores like this laundromat.

White baseball teams traveled around, too. But it was much harder for black teams. In the early 1900s, in towns all across America, white people and black people were kept apart. There were schools for white kids and schools for black kids. There were hotels for white people and restaurants, too. Lots of stores had signs like the one in the photo.

When a black team got to a town, they looked for a black hotel. If there wasn't one, they camped out next to the baseball field. Or they slept on the team bus. Sometimes they weren't allowed to use public bathrooms. Sometimes they weren't even allowed to use the locker rooms at a stadium! It wasn't fair. But the players kept going because they loved baseball.

Z-Z-Z

John Henry Lloyd

Ty Cobb

Every now and then, black teams played against white teams. In 1911, one black team played a few games against the Detroit Tigers, a major-league team. After the games, the famous Detroit hitter, Ty Cobb, had a series batting average of .370. A great black player named **John Henry Lloyd** had a series batting average of .500! He had gotten a hit every other time he went up to bat.

In a book I read for my report, there were stats that showed how all-black teams did against white major-league teams. Over the years, there were about 438 of these games. The major-league teams won 129 games. The black teams won 309.

Rube Foster was a great pitcher. He is also known as the "Father of the Negro Leagues." That's because in 1920, Rube Foster had an idea. There were lots of black baseball teams. So why not start an all-black baseball league? With a league, players could make more money.

Rube Foster

Let's start our own league!

NEGRO NATIONAL

Rube Foster called his new league the Negro
National League. There were eight teams in it. In
1923, more than 400,000 fans came to Negro
National League games. Rube's idea had worked!
Rube Foster became the manager of one of the
Negro National League teams. The team was called
the Chicago American Giants.
Rube smoked a pipe. He used his
pipe to blow smoke signals.
That's how he called the
plays from the dugout.

STEAL
BUNT

LEAGUE

Rube told his players to play "fast" baseball, or "tricky" baseball. He wanted them to bunt, steal bases, and slide. Rube's team was so popular in Chicago that sometimes they got a bigger crowd than the Cubs or White Sox.

Today there is a museum in Kansas City called the Negro Leagues Baseball Museum. I got information from them for my report. Someday I want to go there.

If a player was tagged out standing up, he had to pay Rube $5.⁰⁰.

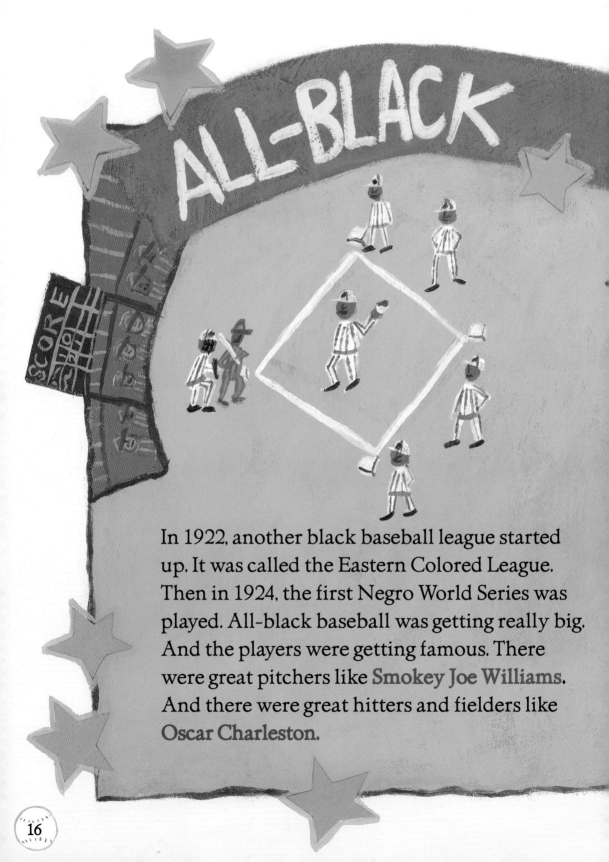

ALL-BLACK

In 1922, another black baseball league started up. It was called the Eastern Colored League. Then in 1924, the first Negro World Series was played. All-black baseball was getting really big. And the players were getting famous. There were great pitchers like Smokey Joe Williams. And there were great hitters and fielders like Oscar Charleston.

WORLD SERIES

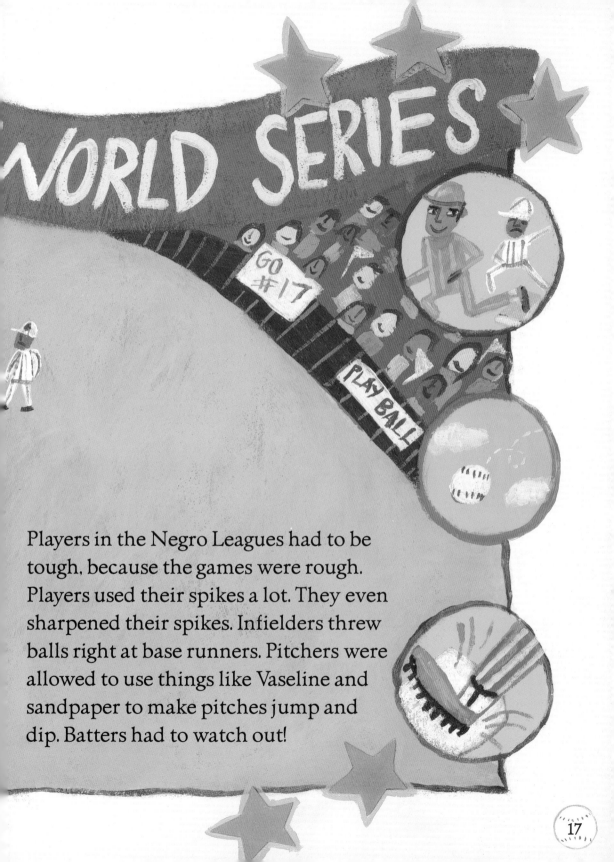

GO #17

PLAY BALL

Players in the Negro Leagues had to be tough, because the games were rough. Players used their spikes a lot. They even sharpened their spikes. Infielders threw balls right at base runners. Pitchers were allowed to use things like Vaseline and sandpaper to make pitches jump and dip. Batters had to watch out!

Three famous Negro League teams in the 1930s were the Homestead Grays, the Pittsburgh Crawfords, and the Kansas City Monarchs. They got the biggest crowds. And they fought over the best players.

From 1937 to 1945 The Homestead Grays won their league championship nine years in a row.

The Kansas City Monarchs were so good, they only had one losing season ever. In 1929, the Kansas City Monarchs put special lights on the back of trucks so they could play games at night. That was six years before the major leagues had night games. But the light posts were only fifty feet high. When a pop fly went above the lights, it was hard to see. And hard to catch!

Josh Gibson

At the Baseball Hall of Fame, I learned about Josh Gibson. He played catcher for the Homestead Grays and the Pittsburgh Crawford He was a home-run hitter, too. He h 962 home runs in his career. Some them were more than 500 feet long They say he once hit a fair ball out Yankee Stadium—all the way out. N one else has ever done that.

Lots of books say Josh Gibson hit 8 home runs in one year. That's more than anybody—even Barry Bonds. Josh Gibson were playing today, he be really famous, but lots of people have never even heard of him.

Yankee Stadium

mes "Cool Papa" Bell played for the
onarchs, the Grays, the Crawfords, and
me other teams, too. He was known as the
stest man in the Negro Leagues. He could
n around the bases in twelve seconds. He
uld steal two bases on one pitch. One of
s roommates said, "Bell was so fast, he
uld get out of bed, turn out the light across
e room, and be back under the covers
fore the lights went out."

GO COOL PAPA

The most famous Negro League player ever was on the Pittsburgh Crawfords and on the Kansas City Monarchs (not at the same time, of course!). His name was Leroy Paige. But everybody called him Satchel. He was born in 1906 in Mobile, Alabama. Satchel got his nickname when he was a kid. He had a job carrying people's bags at the train station. He carried so many bags at once, people said he looked like a "satchel tree."

Satchel got to be such a big star that he even had his own plane.

Satchel Paige was a superstar pitcher. They say that he was so sure of himself, he would tell the outfielders to take a break and sit down while he pitched. I don't know if that's true. But it is definitely true that Satchel Paige was great.

The Great
Satchell Paige

I saw this picture of Satchel at the Hall of Fame. I tried to pitch like this, but I fell over backwards.

'TIME FOR A CHANGE

Finally, in 1947, baseball changed. By then, more and more white people thought it wasn't fair that black players couldn't be in the major leagues. (I don't know why it took them so long to figure that out.)

A man named Branch Rickey was the president of the Brooklyn Dodgers. He also thought it was wrong to keep blacks out of the major leagues, so he decided to do something about it. Branch Rickey started looking for a black player for the Dodgers. But he kept it a secret. He searched long and hard.

Jackie Robinson and Branch Rickey

The player he chose was Jackie Robinson. He was a 27-year-old rookie shortstop for the Kansas City Monarchs. There were other black baseball players who were better than Jackie was. Still, Branch Rickey thought Jackie was the right man.

Why was Jackie picked? Maybe it was because he cared so much about black people getting treated fairly. And keeping black players off teams wasn't fair. Branch Rickey told Jackie that people would yell and curse at him, and that the other players would be mean. Even his teammates might treat him badly. Jackie said, "I'm ready to take the chance."

1947

B

Dodgers

JACKIE ROBINSON
ROOKIE OF THE YEAR

On April 15, 1947, Jackie Robinson put on a Dodgers
uniform and played against the Boston Braves. The
Dodgers won 5 to 3. Branch Rickey was right. Jackie
Robinson's first season was hard. Pitchers hit him with
pitches. Base runners spiked him. Still, Jackie was voted
Rookie of the Year and the Dodgers won the pennant in
1947. In 1949, Jackie was the National League MVP. He
played for the Dodgers for ten years.

At the Baseball Hall of Fame, I saw Jackie Robinson's Dodgers warm-up jacket. I also read one of the hate letters that was sent to Jackie. It was horrible.

My grandpa remembers listening to Jackie Robinson's first major-league game on the radio. Grandpa says it was a very important day and everybody knew it.

"...and Jackie Robinson is up at bat..."

Larry Doby with the Indians manager Lou Boudreau

Roy Campanella

After Jackie, more and more black players got into the major leagues. **Larry Doby** joined the Cleveland Indians a few months after Jackie Robinson became a Dodger. **Roy Campanella** joined the Brooklyn Dodgers in 1949.

Satchel Paige also made it to the major leagues. He joined the Cleveland Indians in 1948. He was 42 years old. He was the oldest rookie ever in the major leagues. He played in the major leagues until he was 59 years old!

Pretty soon, fans stopped coming to all-black baseball games. That's because all the best players like Jackie and Satchel were playing in the major leagues. By the 1960s, more and more black teams went out of business. The Indianapolis Clowns were one of the last Negro League teams around.

SPORTING NEWS
NEGRO BALL FIGHTS
BRAVELY FOR LIFE
AGAINST BIG ODDS

In 1962, Jackie Robinson was voted into the Baseball Hall of Fame. He was the first black player in the Hall of Fame. Then Roy Campanella was voted into the Hall of Fame in 1969. But there were still no Negro League stars in the Hall of Fame. Some people thought the Negro Leagues didn't count.

Ted Williams

In 1966, the famous Ted Williams made a speech. It was the day he got into the Hall of Fame himself. He wanted the great Negro League players to be in the Hall of Fame, too.

In 1971, it happened. Satchel Paige was voted into the Hall of Fame. The year after that, Josh Gibson was voted in. Today there are more than fifteen Negro League players in the National Baseball Hall of Fame.

JACK ROOSEVELT ROBINSON

BROOKLYN N.L. 1947 TO 1956
LEADING N.L. BATTER IN 1949. HOLDS
FIELDING MARK FOR SECOND BASEMAN
PLAYING IN 150 OR MORE GAMES WITH .992.
LED N.L. IN STOLEN BASES IN 1947 AND
1949. MOST VALUABLE PLAYER IN 1949.
LIFETIME BATTING AVERAGE .311. JOINT
RECORD HOLDER FOR MOST DOUBLE PLAYS
BY SECOND BASEMAN, 137 IN 1951.
LED SECOND BASEMEN IN DOUBLE
PLAYS 1949-50-51-52.

LEROY ROBERT PAIGE
"SATCHEL"
NEGRO LEAGUES   1926-1947
CLEVELAND A.L.   1948-1949
ST. LOUIS A.L.   1951-1953
KANSAS CITY A.L.   1965
PAIGE WAS ONE OF THE GREATEST STARS
TO PLAY IN THE NEGRO BASEBALL LEAGUES.
THRILLED MILLIONS OF PEOPLE AND WON
HUNDREDS OF GAMES. STRUCK OUT 21 MAJOR
LEAGUERS IN AN EXHIBITION GAME. HELPED
PITCH CLEVELAND INDIANS TO THE 1948
PENNANT IN HIS FIRST BIG LEAGUE YEAR
AT AGE 42. HIS PITCHING WAS A LEGEND
AMONG MAJOR LEAGUE HITTERS.

Here are Jackie Robinson's plaque and
Satchel Paige's plaque.

NEGRO LEAGUES EXHIBIT

Dodgers

Now whenever people visit the Hall of Fame, they can
see the plaques of the Negro League players. And they
can see the exhibit about the Negro Leagues, just like I
did. That way, maybe more people will know about the
all-black teams and all of the great players. Before I went
to the Hall of Fame, I had never heard of them. But now
I will never forget them.

Emily—
    You hit a home run with this
report. Great job! Have you ever
watched Ken Burns' TV documentary
series on baseball? One of the
episodes is about the Negro Leagues.
It's called "Shadow Ball" – I know
that you would find it very
interesting.

                        Ms. Brandt